DISCARD

Influential Presidents

Franklin D. Roosevelt

by Martha London

www.focusreaders.com

Copyright © 2023 by Focus Readers®, Lake Elmo, MN 55042. All rights reserved. No part of this book may be reproduced or utilized in any form or by any means without written permission from the publisher.

Focus Readers is distributed by North Star Editions: sales@northstareditions.com | 888-417-0195

Produced for Focus Readers by Red Line Editorial.

Photographs ©: FDR Presidential Library and Museum, cover, 1; Shutterstock Images, 4, 13, 22; AP Images, 7, 8, 11, 14, 19, 20–21, 27, 29; World History Archive/Alamy, 17; JS/AP Images, 25

Library of Congress Cataloging-in-Publication Data
Names: London, Martha, author.
Title: Franklin D. Roosevelt / Martha London.
Description: Lake Elmo, MN : Focus Readers, [2023] | Series: Influential presidents | Includes bibliographical references and index. | Audience: Grades 2-3
Identifiers: LCCN 2022030288 (print) | LCCN 2022030289 (ebook) | ISBN 9781637394663 (hardcover) | ISBN 9781637395035 (paperback) | ISBN 9781637395745 (ebook pdf) | ISBN 9781637395400 (hosted ebook)
Subjects: LCSH: Roosevelt, Franklin D. (Franklin Delano), 1882-1945--Juvenile literature. | Presidents--United States--Biography--Juvenile literature. | New Deal, 1933-1939--Juvenile literature. | United States--Politics and government--1933-1945--Juvenile literature.
Classification: LCC E807 .L69 2023 (print) | LCC E807 (ebook) | DDC 973.917092 [B]--dc23/eng/20220628
LC record available at https://lccn.loc.gov/2022030288
LC ebook record available at https://lccn.loc.gov/2022030289

Printed in the United States of America
Mankato, MN
012023

About the Author

Martha London is a writer and educator. She lives in Minnesota with her cat.

Table of Contents

CHAPTER 1
Nothing to Fear 5

CHAPTER 2
Working for Change 9

CHAPTER 3
The New Deal 15

ISSUE SPOTLIGHT
Social Security 20

CHAPTER 4
A Nation at War 23

Focus on Franklin D. Roosevelt • 28
Glossary • 30
To Learn More • 31
Index • 32

Chapter 1

Nothing to Fear

In 1933, the United States was facing hard times. The **Great Depression** had ruined the **economy**. Millions of people lost their jobs. Many people lost their homes. Some people went hungry.

 **Unemployed people wait in line for free soup during the Great Depression.**

Franklin D. Roosevelt was the new president. On his first day in office, he gave a speech. It was **broadcast** on the radio.

Roosevelt told people not to be afraid. He said the Great Depression would not last forever. People needed to stay hopeful.

Roosevelt gave many speeches on the radio. These speeches became known as "fireside chats."

 Roosevelt (center) takes his oath of office in March 1933.

Roosevelt said he would increase the power of the government. That way, the government could give people the help they needed.

Chapter 2

Working for Change

Franklin D. Roosevelt was born on January 30, 1882. He grew up in New York. His family was wealthy. They paid for private teachers and expensive schools. Roosevelt went to college to be a lawyer.

 A young Franklin D. Roosevelt plays with a bow and arrow.

In 1910, Roosevelt ran for the New York Senate. He won. He was only 28 years old at the time. Roosevelt hoped to make big changes. And in 1913, he got the chance. President Woodrow Wilson asked Roosevelt to work with the US Navy. A year later,

Did You Know?

In 1921, Roosevelt got a serious disease. He lost the ability to walk. So, he started using a wheelchair.

 Roosevelt works at his desk in the New York Senate.

World War I (1914–1918) began. Roosevelt wanted to make sure sailors were ready. He helped improve the navy's ships. He also helped make the navy larger.

In 1928, New York voters elected Roosevelt as governor. The next year, the Great Depression began. Many people lost their jobs. They also lost money that was in banks. Roosevelt created programs to help New York's banks. He also lowered **taxes** for farmers.

Did You Know?

During the Great Depression, many people could not afford to stay in their homes. So, they lived in tents or shacks.

 Huge dust storms ruined many farms during the Great Depression.

Roosevelt's programs were popular with voters. He was reelected in 1930. During his second **term** as governor, Roosevelt created another program. It gave money to people who had lost their jobs.

13

Chapter 3

The New Deal

Franklin D. Roosevelt's programs in New York were working. But much of the country continued to struggle. Roosevelt ran for president in 1932. He ran against President Herbert Hoover.

Roosevelt waves to supporters during the 1932 presidential election.

15

Hoover thought **aid** should come from local governments and companies. But those groups also lacked money. As a result, Hoover's **policies** did not help many people. Roosevelt had different ideas. He believed the US government should help people directly.

Voters elected Roosevelt in 1932. He made many changes in his first 100 days as president. His programs were known as the New Deal. The first thing he did was

 During the Great Depression, many people lost their homes and lived in shacks.

help banks. Roosevelt changed the rules that banks had to follow. These rules helped people trust the banks again.

Next, Roosevelt made programs to help workers. These programs gave jobs and **income** to people.

17

Workers built dams. They planted trees. They made parks. Their work helped improve the country.

Most people liked Roosevelt's programs. Voters elected him again in 1936. During his second term, Roosevelt raised taxes on rich people. He also raised taxes on large businesses. These

When Roosevelt took office, more than 13 million people did not have jobs.

 One of Roosevelt's programs hired workers to build new roads.

taxes helped pay for the New Deal programs.

The economy slowly started to improve. But the United States faced another threat. World War II (1939–1945) began during Roosevelt's second term.

ISSUE SPOTLIGHT

Social Security

In the early 1930s, most states did not give aid to people who were too old to work. And most states did not help people who had lost their jobs. As a result, many people had no way to pay for the things they needed.

In 1935, Roosevelt signed the Social Security Act. This law gave money to older people. It also gave money to people who could not find jobs. Social Security still exists today. Many people depend on it.

Roosevelt (seated) signs the Social Security Act into law.

Chapter 4

A Nation at War

Franklin D. Roosevelt won a third term in 1940. At the time, the United States was not involved in World War II. But in 1941, Japan attacked a US base in Hawaii. The United States was now at war.

More than 2,400 Americans died during the Japanese attack on Hawaii.

23

Soldiers needed guns, tanks, and planes. So, the US government spent huge amounts of money on the war. As a result, many New Deal programs ended. But many new jobs were created. For example, millions of women went to work in factories. They helped make weapons and supplies.

Did You Know?

Roosevelt was the only president to be elected four times.

 Women build an airplane cockpit in 1942.

The war continued for several years. Roosevelt won a fourth term in 1944. However, he had been sick for a long time. Roosevelt died on April 12, 1945. A few months later, World War II finally ended.

Before he died, Roosevelt helped create the United Nations. This group is made up of countries from around the world. They work together for peace.

Roosevelt is best known for leading the United States through the Great Depression

The United Nations formed in 1945. At the time, only 51 countries were members. Today, more than 190 countries are members.

 Roosevelt (center) meets with other world leaders in early 1945.

and World War II. Few presidents have accomplished as much as Roosevelt did.

27

FOCUS ON
Franklin D. Roosevelt

Write your answers on a separate piece of paper.

1. Write a sentence that describes the main ideas of Chapter 3.

2. Roosevelt believed the government should help people directly. Do you agree? Why or why not?

3. When did the Great Depression begin?
    - **A.** 1929
    - **B.** 1932
    - **C.** 1945

4. What might have happened without Roosevelt's New Deal programs?
    - **A.** More banks would have opened.
    - **B.** More people would have run out of money.
    - **C.** More people would have found jobs.

5. What does **wealthy** mean in this book?

*His family was **wealthy**. They paid for private teachers and expensive schools.*

    A. having lots of money
    B. doing well in school
    C. unable to travel far

6. What does **accomplished** mean in this book?

*Roosevelt is best known for leading the United States through the Great Depression and World War II. Few presidents have **accomplished** as much as Roosevelt did.*

    A. made many mistakes
    B. changed people's minds
    C. met a goal successfully

Answer key on page 32.

Glossary

aid
Money that the government gives to a person or group to help pay for education, health care, or other services.

broadcast
Sent out radio or TV signals.

economy
A system of goods, services, money, and jobs.

Great Depression
A time when many people lost their jobs and homes. It lasted from the late 1920s to the late 1930s.

income
Money earned from a job.

policies
Rules created by a government.

taxes
Money the government collects from people and companies to pay for services.

term
The amount of time a person can serve after being elected.

To Learn More

BOOKS

Glenn, Dusk. *Franklin Delano Roosevelt: World War II President*. New York: Scholastic, 2021.

Gunderson, Megan M. *Franklin D. Roosevelt*. Minneapolis: Abdo Publishing, 2021.

Maupin, Melissa. *Franklin D. Roosevelt*. Mankato, MN: The Child's World, 2020.

NOTE TO EDUCATORS

Visit **www.focusreaders.com** to find lesson plans, activities, links, and other resources related to this title.

Index

B
banks, 12, 17

E
economy, 5, 19

F
farmers, 12
fireside chats, 6

G
governor, 12–13
Great Depression, 5–6, 12, 26

H
Hoover, Herbert, 15–16

N
New Deal, 16, 19, 24
New York Senate, 10

S
Social Security, 20

T
taxes, 12, 18–19

U
United Nations, 26
US Navy, 10–11

W
Wilson, Woodrow, 10
World War I, 11
World War II, 19, 23, 25, 27

Answer Key: **1.** Answers will vary; **2.** Answers will vary; **3.** A; **4.** B; **5.** A; **6.** C